Wars & Treaties

1815-1914

Wars & Treaties

1815-1914

Arthur Ponsonby

Vij Books India Pvt Ltd
New Delhi (India)

Published by

Vij Books India Pvt Ltd
(Publishers, Distributors & Importers)
2/19, Ansari Road
Delhi – 110 002
Phones: 91-11-43596460, 91-11-47340674
Mobile: 98110 94883
e-mail: contact@vijpublishing.com
www.vijbooks.in

Copyright © 2022,

ISBN: 978-93-93499-44-8

Contents

DEMOCRACY AND DIPLOMACY

(3s. 6d. net)

BY
ARTHUR PONSONBY

"It is the completest statement of the case for the democratic control of foreign affairs which has been published, and contains a mass of facts whose value cannot be exaggerated. We owe Mr. Ponsonby a great debt for this work."—*Labour Leader.*

"... Mr. Ponsonby's main contention is one which may and should receive the hearty assent of many who disagree with him in detail. He strongly urges the necessity in dealing with foreign affairs of ensuring the co-operation and approval of the great mass of the people. He is manifestly quite right."—The late LORD CROMER in The *Spectator.*

REBELS AND REFORMERS

(6s. net)

BY
ARTHUR & DOROTHEA PONSONBY

Savonarola—William the Silent—Tycho Brahe—Cervantes—
Giordano Bruno—Grotius—Voltaire—Hans Andersen—
Mazzini—W. Lloyd Garrison—Thoreau—Tolstoy

"Mr. and Mrs. Ponsonby's book is intended for children or for those who are too busy to read books in many volumes. But the interest of it lies not in the necessarily short and simple narratives giving the story rather than the ideas, although these are done clearly and with spirit, but in the reflections which lie about those stories and lodge here and there in the reader's mind. Like all books worth reading this one is the outcome of a mass of judgments and beliefs which may be very briefly expressed in the work itself, but lend it the gift which in the case of human beings we call personality."—*The Times Literary Supplement.*

"The story of these twelve lives is told in these pages—and told with a most enticing simplicity and the happiest taste—in the hope of redressing the balance between men of action and men of thought, and of showing that this type of character and achievement can be made just as interesting to the young as the more conventional hero of the history book.... This book is more especially for the young, but it will be a delight also to grown-up readers."—*The Nation.*

"The biographies are always well simplified and written in a clear and pointed way. They are accompanied by portraits, which add not a little to the work's attractiveness as a book unusually well fitted to the needs of young readers who are beginning to take an interest in history."—*The Scotsman.*

INTRODUCTION

A GROWING number of people are devoting their attention to a closer study of foreign affairs. Many of them may not have the opportunity to read the larger volumes of histories; and, indeed, even if they had, they would find their choice of books very much restricted when they came to the more recent period of European and world history, although in the last year or so the gap has to some extent been filled up by several interesting studies of international politics in the nineteenth century. Some knowledge of this period is essential if we are to understand the full significance of the events of to-day, and if we are to form any helpful opinion of the course to be pursued in future.

Historians often take for granted that their readers already have some general knowledge of the groundwork of events and they build up their structure of criticism, their delineation of policy and tendencies, and their survey of international problems on the assumption that the scaffolding has been erected. But often it has not, and then history, more especially the complex tangle of international history, becomes difficult to grasp. It may therefore serve some useful purpose if a few poles of scaffolding representing the dates and outline of conflicts and agreements between nations can be supplied in a very brief and easily intelligible form, a presentment of the bare record of facts which may be useful for reference.

During the last hundred years war has been a more common occurrence in international intercourse than most people realize. The forty-two records of wars tabled in these pages do not cover the whole ground. They are the chief conflicts, or the conflicts fraught with the most serious consequences, but they are by no means the only occasions on which there was fighting in the world. Revolutions, unless they led to international war, are not mentioned, neither are expeditions such as the advance on Llassa, the Chitral expedition, the Indian frontier wars, the Kaffir wars, the Somaliland expeditions, the revolt of the Herreroes in German West Africa or the French expeditions in Morocco: the wars between the states of South America, with two exceptions, have also been omitted. But the list as it stands, is striking enough and may suffice to make the student inquire further into the circumstances which produced this almost unceasing strife.

The causes are epitomized in the fewest possible words and the occasion is separated from the cause. Causes of wars are very seldom remembered and are not very easily discovered in the perusal of histories. The occasion is sometimes mistaken for the cause, whereas it may often be merely a pretext. The occasion of a war has not infrequently been a comparatively trivial incident, whereas the cause can be traced to the gradual development of friction for which divergence of policies or conflict of ambitions may have been responsible. The trivial incident, or even an incident of a more serious nature, may pass off without fatal consequences if no friction exists between the nations and there is a general atmosphere of amicable understanding. Where, on the contrary, relations are strained it requires but a very small spark to light up a conflagration. It is important therefore to detach the occasion from the cause.

Causes of war in the nineteenth century differ to some extent from those of previous centuries. The elemental combative passion of man expressing itself in fierce racial animosities is far less noticeable. Religious differences do not figure so positively as a reason for conflict. Dynastic ambitions linger on and still play a formidable part, even after 1815, but not with the same unashamed and aggressive arrogance as in bygone centuries. Nationalist aspirations begin to assert themselves, and the waves of revolutionary exasperation with outworn systems ofdespotic government have made those very governments combat that spirit by force of arms. As the century proceeds, and the wonderful inventions for rapid transit and communication develop, the most noticeable element in war-making is the commercial or colonial ambition of governments fostered largely by the pressure of financial interests and declaring itself under the name of Empire. This policy of competitive imperial expansion in the newly accessible regions of the globe will be found to constitute the most frequent cause of dispute, of jealousy, and of suspicion between nations. The pretext will vary, the excuse will be presented under plausible guises for popular consumption, but the ultimate cause, the fundamental origin will be the same. Imperialism economic in its origin is fostered largely by an exaggerated spirit of nationalism.

The remarkable extent of Empire expansion in the latter part of the nineteenth century is best illustrated by the following figures:—

Acquisitions of Territory

To the British Empire 1870–1900: 4,754,000 square miles; 88,000,000 population.

To France 1884–1900: 3,583,580 square miles; 36,553,000 population.

To Germany 1884–1900: 1,026,220 square miles; 16,687,100 population.

But perhaps the chief and most frequent cause of war is war itself. In the Balkan Peninsula—where, whenever the fighting has ceased, nothing approaching a satisfactory settlement has ever been concluded—this is specially true. Eight or nine of the wars recorded concern the Balkans. Or take the Crimean War. Sir Spencer Walpole says:

"From 1856 to 1878 the Continent of Europe was afflicted with five great wars—the Franco-Austrian War of 1859; the Danish of 1864; the Austro-Prussian of 1860; the Franco-German of 1870 and the Russo-Turkish of 1878: all of which can be lineally traced to the war of 1854," and one at least of those wars, as we know, sowed the seeds of future war. The war that is concluded by a dictated peace, the war that leaves a sense of grievance and unsatisfied though legitimate claims, the war that inspires a lasting desire for revenge inevitably leads to future war. Wars are never aggressive but always defensive on the part of those who are responsible for waging them. Wars are never defensive but always aggressive on the part of those against whom they are waged. The Ministers and monarchs do the quarrelling, the people believe the version they are told and obey. The people do the fighting and make the sacrifice, the Ministers and monarchs do the treaty-making without consulting them. The people's part is one of valiance, endurance, and suffering; the part of the Ministers and monarchs is one too often marred by failure and frequently disfigured by intrigue and deception.

Cast your eye through these forty-two very brief records of wars. Think of the valour, the determination, and the heroism of the people, be they soldiers or civilians. Consider the noble part played by those who without question obeyed what they were led to believe was their country's call. And then look on the other side at the results—the ineptitude of the statesmen, the patched-up treaties, the worthless agreements, the wars that led to further wars, the failure to secure a settlement after the soldier had done his part, and the unnecessary prolongation of conflicts when agreement might have been reached by the exercise of a little wisdom and foresight. The contrast is remarkable between the actions on the battlefield and the intrigue in the council chamber. Blood has been spilt, lives lost, and victories won often without any positive advantage being gained in the final result.

The wars are arranged according to date. Some were long-drawn-out struggles, others sharp conflicts of a few months. The number of men engaged in any battle and the casualties if they could be tabulated would no doubt seem comparatively small to our modern eyes. The total loss of life in the Crimean War amounted to about 600,000 men.1 An estimate of the loss in killed and wounded in some of the other great battles may be given as follows: Solferino (1859), 31,500; Chickamauga (1863), 35,100; Gettysburg (1863), 37,000; Königrätz (1866), 26,894; Vionville (1870), 32,800; Gravelotte (1870), 30,000; Plevna (1877), 19,000;2 The Boer War (1899–1902): British losses, 28,603; Boers killed, 4,000, prisoners 41,000;3 Mukden (1905), 131,000.

1 *The Cambridge Modern History*, vol. xii

2 An article in *Current History*, by General Duryee, of the U.S.A. Army.

3 *Encyclopædia Britannica.*

Wars to the generation that experiences them are unmixed evils engendering hatred and evil passions and bringing in their train loss, suffering, destruction, and impoverishment, all of which are acutely felt. The succeeding generation inherit their consequences in the shape of high taxation and the attempts to mend and reconstruct the dislocated national life. The horror has gone but the memory remains. To the succeeding generation they become episodes read of in the cold pages of history, and then at last they fade into mere names—a battle with a vaguely remembered date.

Each war is terminated by a treaty. The main provisions of a few additional treaties which were not concluded after wars are also given. In but few instances have war treaties been observed, and in several cases they were not worth the paper they were written on. Treaties are signed and ratified by statesmen without the sanction or approval, and sometimes without the knowledge, of their people. The statesmen enter the council chamber as individuals bent on securing advantages at other people's expense, and ready by bargain and intrigue to attain their ends. These instruments therefore are expressions of temporary expediency sometimes exacted after defeat, sometimes the result of compromise and generally inconclusive. If treaties are to become sacred obligations founded on international justice and respected not merely by changing governments but by whole nations, the spirit in which they are drawn up and the method by which they are concluded must be radically altered. The existence of secret treaties and engagements has proved to be one of the gravest dangers to European peace.

There are a large number of conventions which have been concluded between nations, by which social intercourse with regard to such matters as post and telegraph is facilitated, and of late years arbitration treaties between one Power and another have multiplied very rapidly. This is the one advance in which the efforts of diplomacy have borne fruit. The important treaty of Arbitration between Great Britain and the United States is the only one of these treaties mentioned in the list. Agreements with regard to the conduct of war have been made, such as the Geneva Convention of 1864 and 1906, and the Hague Declarations of 1899 and 1907, but they have proved to a large extent futile.

Treaties are generally concluded for an undefined period, and lapse owing to deliberate breach or altered circumstances. But no people, and it may safely be said no government, was precisely aware which of the innumerable treaties were still in force, and what actually in given circumstances its obligations were.

There may be many instances in which a nation may look back with pride at the victory of its arms and the achievements of its generals. There are but few instances in which a nation can look back with pride at the advantages gained by treaties of peace and at the achievements of its diplomatists. From the Treaty of Vienna, 1815, to the Treaty of Bukarest, 1913, the record of so-called settlements is not one to inspire confidence in the efficacy of warfare or in the methods of diplomacy.

After the termination of the Napoleonic Wars in 1815 there were great hopes of an era of peace. But two antagonistic elements existed in Europe which were bound sooner or later to come into open conflict. On the one hand the French Revolution had engendered in the peoples a spirit of unrest, of discontent, of impatience with the unfettered monarchical system, and at the same time confidence in their power and hope of success in the destruction of tyranny and arbitrary government. It was in fact the rise of democracy. On the other side the despotic governments were ready to co-operate, and, under the guidance of Metternich, endeavour to repress and exterminate the movement for the establishment of constitutional government, and for the expression of nationalist and democratic aspirations. Two waves of revolution passed over Europe in 1830 and 1848, and by the middle of the century the reactionaries could no longer hold their own, and many states had been freed from despotism and oppression.

In the latter part of the century, however, as has already been pointed out, fresh causes for war arose in the competitive ambition of governments for imperial expansion. Wars became more frequent and extended into remote regions of the world which had become accessible. There are forty-seven wars mentioned in these records; of these thirteen took place before the Crimean War, which is about the middle of the period, and thirty-three after. In twenty-one out of the forty-five wars Great Britain was either directly or indirectly concerned as a belligerent. There were only two wars in which Christian nations were not primarily involved.

It must be remembered that in no country had the peoples any voice in the determination of policy so far as international affairs were concerned. While for brevity's sake the usual phraseology is adopted, and such expressions used as "France decided," "Russia refused," "Italy intended," etc., etc., in no case does the name of the country mean the people or indeed anything more than a monarch and a few statesmen. Although constitutional monarchy became established during the period in many countries, and with it, parliamentary government, the idea of diplomacy, foreign policy, international engagements, and treaties being under parliamentary supervision and control, had not yet been suggested.

The solution of the vast problem of the avoidance of war in the future, if it rests alone on the wisdom of sovereigns and statesmen, is not likely, judging by the experience of the past, to be reached very rapidly. In the meanwhile a careful examination of the events of recent history is a necessary preparation for all who want to dispel the strange but prevalent delusion that force of arms settles international disputes, and this record may be useful as a manual for reference.

THE GREEK WAR

1821–1828

Belligerents:

Greece and later Russia, France and Great Britain.
Turkey.

Cause:

Nationalist aspirations had been growing in Greece ever since the French Revolution. These were encouraged by an intellectual revival and commercial development. The tyranny and cruel oppression of Turkish misgovernment under Sultan Mahmud gradually inflamed public opinion.

Occasion:

The HetæriaPhilike, a secret society, inaugurated the rebellion. The first move was made in Moldavia, where it completely failed. This was followed by a revolt in the Morea and the islands of the Ægean and subsequently in Central Greece.

Course of the War:

There were wholesale massacres on both sides, notably the destruction by the Turks of the inhabitants of Chios. The Turks were unable to suppress the revolt. The Greeks under Kolokotrones exhausted the Turkish army, and assistance was sought by the Sultan from Mehemet Ali, of Egypt, who in 1823 conquered Crete and defeated the Greeks at Psara. The Egyptians and Turks entered Morea. Missolonghi fell after a year's siege, and the garrison in the Acropolis at Athens surrendered in June 1827. By a treaty signed at London in July 1827 Great Britain, France, and Russia decided to intervene as mediators. The Turks rejected mediation. The victory of the allied fleets at Navarino took place on October 20 1827.

Political Result:

By the *Treaty of Adrianople*, September 1829 (see also p. 17) Greece became autonomous under the supreme sovereignty of the Sultan. Shortly afterwards the Powers agreed that Greece should be established as an absolutely independent kingdom, but without Crete or Samos, and with a frontier line drawn from the mouth of the River

Achelous to a spot near Thermopylæ. Prince Leopold of Saxe-Coburg accepted the crown, but renounced it after a few months. Prince Otho of Bavaria accepted it in February 1833. After a revolution in 1862 he was succeeded by Prince George of Denmark in 1863, the father of King Constantine who was deposed in 1917.

Remarks:

Greece was confined within far too narrow limits, with which she could not rest contented. The enmity between Russia and Turkey was in no way mitigated, and Russian ambitions remained unsatisfied.

RUSSO-TURKISH WAR

1828–1829

Belligerents:

Russia.
Turkey.

Cause:

By the Treaty of London, July 1827, Great Britain, Russia, and France undertook to put an end to the conflict in the East, which had arisen out of the Greek struggle for independence. After the victory of Navarino, Canning died and Great Britain was inactive. By the *Treaty of Akerman*, October 1826, the points of contention between Russia and Turkey had been settled in Russia's favour. But the Russian Government ardently desired a contest with Turkey.

Occasion:

The Sultan Mahmud issued a proclamation which was a direct challenge to Russia, and followed it by a levy of troops and the expulsion of Christians from Constantinople. On April 26, 1828, Russia replied by declaring war.

Course of the War:

The Russians occupied the Roumanian principalities and crossed the Danube. At first the Turks had considerable successes in the Dobrudja, and the Russians, who suffered enormous losses, were only able to capture Varna. Reserves were brought up during the winter. After fierce resistance the Turks were routed near Shumla. In July 1829 the Russians crossed the Balkans, the fleet co-operated in the Black Sea, and the army began to march on Constantinople. In Asia, Kars and Erzeroum having fallen into the Russian hands, the Sultan yielded.

Political Result:

By the *Treaty of Adrianople*, September 14, 1829, Russian ascendancy in the principalities of the Danube was permanently assured, and the whole of the Caucasus was converted into Russian territory. The Straits were declared free and open to merchant ships of all Powers. The Turkish Government gave its adhesion to the Treaty of London regulating the Greek frontier.

Remarks:

Russia's hold over Turkey was greatly strengthened, but the establishment of an absolutely independent kingdom in Greece was finally secured.

WAR BETWEEN HOLLAND AND BELGIUM

1830–1839

Belligerents:

> Holland.
> Belgium, France, Great Britain.

Cause:

The Kingdom of the Netherlands was set up by the Congress of Vienna in 1815, but from the first there was discord between the two states of the kingdom. King William was a Dutchman and a Protestant. Holland, although the smaller of the two states, had a permanent majority in the Chamber. Public offices and appointments were filled by Dutchmen. The hatred of Dutch rule grew, and with it a desire for separation.

Occasion:

The success of the French Revolution of 1830 led to an outbreak in Brussels, and Belgian insurgents fought against the Dutch soldiers. The Powers met in London, and Belgium was declared a separate kingdom. Leopold of Saxe-Coburg was offered the crown and entered Brussels as King of the Belgians on June 21, 1831; at the same time the Dutch prepared for an invasion.

Course of the War:

On August 9, 1831, the Belgians were routed in an encounter with the Dutch, but on the intervention of the French army King William withdrew. The Conference in London drew up a treaty, but King William refused to come to terms and retained possession of Antwerp. In November a combined British and French fleet sailed for the coast of Holland, and a French army laid siege to Antwerp. The Dutch garrison capitulated on December 23, 1831, and the town was handed over to the Belgians and the French troops withdrew. Still the Dutch refused to yield and held two forts which enabled them to command the navigation of the Scheldt. Not till March 1838 did Holland signify her readiness to accept the treaty.

Political Result:

The Conference throughout had endeavoured to come to an agreement; Austria, Prussia, and Russia sympathized with Holland; but eventually the final *Treaty of London* was signed on April 19, 1839. Luxemburg was divided, and also the district of Maestricht. The Scheldt was declared open to the commerce of both countries. The national debt was divided, and the five Powers guaranteed the independence and neutrality of Belgium.

Remarks:

As independent states the two countries lived side by side amicably. The neutrality of Belgium was reaffirmed in 1870 on the outbreak of the Franco-German War.

Leopold was succeeded in 1865 by his son Leopold II, under whose sovereignty the Congo Free State was placed in 1885. King Albert succeeded his uncle in 1909.

WAR IN PORTUGAL AND SPAIN

1830–1839

Belligerents:

> Followers of Don Miguel.
> Portuguese Constitutionalists.
> Spaniards.
> Carlists.
> and for a period France and Great Britain.

Cause:

Don Miguel, the head of the reactionary party, was betrothed to Donna Maria, daughter of Pedro of Brazil. In 1828, disregarding his professions of loyalty to the Constitution, he declared himself King of Portugal. The Constitutionalists, who were adherents of Donna Maria, were crushed. She received no assistance from outside to deal with the usurper.

In Spain Don Carlos, the King's brother, was the representative of the reactionary party. King Ferdinand, before his death, issued the Pragmatic Sanction, which enabled his daughter to succeed to the throne. The King was weak and unpopular, and Don Carlos had a great following in Spain.

Occasion:

In 1830 Great Britain and France demanded satisfaction for the attacks on their subjects in Lisbon, and their squadrons appeared in the Tagus. Great Britain obtained an indemnity and an apology: the French admiral carried off the best ships of Don Miguel's navy. In 1831 Pedro came over from Brazil and raised troops for the reconquest of Portugal, which began in the following year. Don Carlos was making common cause with Don Miguel when the King of Spain died in 1833, and his child Isabella was declared Queen, with Christina, his wife, as Regent. Rebellion broke out, and Don Carlos was proclaimed King in several provinces.

Course of the War:

Don Pedro captured Oporto, but was besieged there for nearly a year. With assistance from outside he overcame the resistance of the enemy and entered Lisbon in July, 1833. A quadruple treaty was signed at London in April 1834, by which Spain and Portugal, assisted by Great Britain and France, engaged to drive both Miguel and Carlos from the Peninsula. A Spanish army marched against Miguel and the British fleet arrived. Miguel renounced the crown, and quitted the Peninsula. Don Carlos was conducted to London, but he escaped and appeared again in Spain at the head of his insurgents in July 1834. He gained several victories, and prepared to march on Madrid. Christina appealed to France for assistance, but Louis Philippe was reluctant to embark on the enterprise and refused. The war continued till at last General Espatero forced back the insurgents, the Carlists turned their arms against one another, and Don Carlos surrendered and crossed the French frontier.

Political Result:

Absolutism was crushed and a more constitutional form of government was established. But the throne of Spain was the subject of further disputes in the future.

Remarks:

This prolonged and barbaric conflict disgraced the Spanish nation. The three Eastern Powers favoured the cause of Don Carlos and reaction. It was the fear of possibly provoking a general war that made France refuse to intervene.

RUSSIAN CAMPAIGN IN POLAND

1831

Belligerents:

Russia.
Poland.

Cause:

By the three partitions of 1772, 1793, and 1795 Poland ceased to exist as an independent state, and Polish territory was divided up between Russia, Prussia, and Austria. But in 1814 the Grand Duchy of Warsaw was established as a separate kingdom subject to the Czar of Russia. The economic and political life was revived and with it antagonism to Russia. In 1828 plans were made for an outbreak, but the opportunity was neglected. The French Revolution of 1830 rekindled the flames.

Occasion:

A revolt broke out in November 1830. An attempt was made to negotiate with the Czar Nicholas, who let it be understood that Poland had but two alternatives, unconditional submission or annihilation. The Polish Government, in January 1831, replied by proclaiming his dethronement. War was unavoidable, and Russian troops crossed the Polish frontier in February.

Course of the War:

The losses sustained by the Russian armies were considerable, but the Poles had to fall back on Warsaw and were defeated at Ostrolenka. Russian reinforcements came up, and on September 8, 1831, the Russian army made its entrance into Warsaw, and the revolt was suppressed.

Political Result:

The Constitution of Poland was abolished: it ceased to be a separate kingdom and became a province of the Russian Empire. The Polish leaders were exiled.

Remarks:

The Poles might have won a gradual development of constitutional liberty without a break with the powerful sovereignty of the Czar; the revolt no doubt was rash and unwise. But, on the other hand, the governments of Western Europe, including Great Britain, who, by the Treaty of Vienna, guaranteed the autonomy of Poland, never lifted a hand on behalf of Polish independence, and acquiesced in its complete absorption by Russia.

THE TURKO-EGYPTIAN WAR

1832–1841

Belligerents:

Turkey and later Prussia, Austria, Russia, and Great Britain.
Egypt.

Cause:

The ambition for extension of power on the part of Mehemet Ali, Viceroy of Egypt.

Occasion:

Unsatisfied with the Island of Crete given to him for his services to the Ottoman Empire, Mehemet Ali sent his son Ibrahim with a force and laid siege to Acre. He was declared a rebel, and the Turkish army entered Syria.

Course of the War:

Syria and Asia Minor were conquered by Ibrahim. Russia offered aid, but on the intervention of France the Sultan was persuaded to make peace, making over to Mehemet Ali Syria and the province of Adena. At the same time, in July 1833, a treaty of defensive alliance was signed at *UnkiarSkelessi* between Russia and Turkey, by which Russia obtained very nearly complete ascendancy at Constantinople. Great Britain desired to maintain the Sultan's power: France befriended Mehemet Ali: both were agreed in checking Russian influence in the Levant. War broke out again. Ibrahim gained a victory at Nissibim in June 1839, and the Turkish fleet surrendered to Mehemet Ali at Alexandria. A quadruple treaty was signed by Great Britain, Russia, Austria, and Prussia, by which it was proposed that Mehemet should have the hereditary government of Egypt, should withdraw from Syria and hold Palestine as a governor under the Porte. The exclusion of France from this agreement roused great public indignation. By the aid of the Allies Mehemet Ali was driven from Syria. Acre was captured by Sir Charles Napier, and Mehemet submitted.

Political Result:

By the final settlement, to which France also agreed, Mehemet Ali abandoned all claim to provinces outside Egypt, undertook to restore the Turkish fleet, and was assured the hereditary possession of Egypt. The Straits were closed to the warships of all nations. This prevented Russia from becoming a Mediterranean Power.

Remarks:

Turkey now became dependent on the protection of Europe. Hopes of internal reform, however, never fructified. The conflicting ambitions of European Powers with regard to the continually shrinking dominions of the Sultan became henceforth an increasing source of friction.

FIRST AFGHAN WAR

1838–1842

Belligerents:

Great Britain and Indian Troops.
Afghanistan.

Cause:

The close proximity of Afghanistan to India necessitated the British Government watching jealously the affairs of that country, and preparing for the possibility of its being brought under the domination of any other Power. Russian intrigues had been throughout a source of suspicion and uneasiness. The British policy was declared to be the maintenance of the integrity and independence of Afghanistan.

Occasion:

The British Government decided to reinstate Shah Shuja, who was a refugee in British territory, DostMahommed being in power at Kabul.

Course of the War:

A British Indian force advanced in March 1838, and entered Kandahar. Shah Shuja was crowned. DostMahommed withdrew, and Kabul was entered. The war was brought to an end, but in November 1841 a revolt broke out in Kabul and there were serious massacres. The British garrison in withdrawing was overwhelmed between Kabul and Jalalabad. Reinforcements, in 1842, forced the Kyber Pass, relieved Jalalabad and occupied Kabul. The army finally evacuated Afghanistan in December 1842.

Political Result:

A ruler imposed on a free people by foreign arms is always unpopular. The Afghans considered that Shah Shuja's rule under the protection of British troops might be fatal to their national independence.

Remarks:

This war has been described as a rash, ill-planned, and hazardous enterprise, and was the immediate cause of further trouble. (See p. <u>58</u>.)

THE OPIUM WAR IN CHINA

1840–1842

Belligerents:

> Great Britain.
> China.

Cause:

The Chinese still held the doctrine that no political relations or dealings should be held with any foreign country. The British Government under Palmerston decided to place trade relations with China on a more satisfactory basis, confusion and annoyance having arisen owing to the expiry of the East India Company's charter. They also resolved to protect the opium traffic in spite of the protests of the Chinese Government. This latter reason overshadowed the others, and the war, which was known as the Opium War, was the subject of heated controversy in England.

Occasion:

The Chinese Government refused to recognize the British Commission or to come to terms on the opium question. Reports in 1839 from Captain Elliot, the British Trade Commissioner, led to the decision of the British Government to send an expedition, and war was declared in 1840.

Course of the War:

The fleet captured Chusan, and in the following year Amoy. Ningpo fell, and in 1842 Chapu, Woosung, and Shanghai shared the same fate. Before Nanking could be captured the Chinese Government proposed terms of peace.

Political Result:

By the *Treaty of Nanking*, August 21, 1842, Hong-kong was formally ceded to the British Crown; Canton, Amoy, Fuchow, Ningpo, and Shanghai were declared open to foreign trade. A war indemnity of twelve million dollars was paid to Great Britain, and subsequent treaties were signed for the regulation of trade.

Remarks:

This was the beginning of the exploitation of China by the Western Powers. It led to further wars, and the opium question continued to agitate public opinion in Great Britain and cause disputes with China for the rest of the century, until the opium trade was finally abolished in 1913.

AMERICAN WAR WITH MEXICO

1846–1848

Belligerents:

The United States of America.
Mexico.

Cause:

Texas seceded from Mexico in 1836. The independence of Texas was recognized by the United States, but the proposal that the new state should be admitted into the Union was declined. A strong support for the annexation of Texas in the interests of slavery grew up, more especially in the Southern states, and in December 1844 resolutions were passed in both Houses, and it was formally enrolled as a new state.

Occasion:

The Mexican Government still claimed Texas as a province, and its annexation by the United States was considered an act of hostility. The Americans had suffered long under continued acts of insult and spoliation on the part of the Mexicans, and were therefore prepared to fight.

Course of the War:

The Americans under Taylor invaded Mexico, won battles at Palo Alto and Resaca and captured Monterey. In 1847 there were more victories, the Mexicans under Santa Anna being everywhere defeated. The Americans entered Mexico City on September 14th. After further fighting peace was proclaimed at Washington in July 1848.

Political Result:

By the *Treaty of Guadalupe-Hidalgo*, February 2, 1848, Mexico ceded the whole of Texas, New Mexico, and Upper California. The United States surrendered their other conquests.

Remarks:

So far as Texas was concerned, the political opinion in the United States was divided, and that division was to become more serious as time went on. On the other hand, Mexico was a troublesome neighbour, and has continued ever since to be the cause of disturbance and dispute.

- 27 -

AUSTRO-HUNGARIAN WAR

1848–1849

Belligerents:

> Hungary.
> Austria, the Southern Slavs and Russia.

Cause:

The fall of Metternich, who had been the champion of despotism and reaction throughout Europe, and the revolutionary spirit which ran through Europe in 1848, created great unrest in the Austro-Hungarian Empire. The Emperor Ferdinand was weak and worthless, and the Magyars were determined not to submit to the domination of autocratic rule in Austria. Jellacic, the Croatian leader, hoped to create a Southern Slav state: he co-operated with the Austrians in opposition to Hungary, and was supported by the Czechs of Bohemia.

Occasion:

Finding it impossible to come to terms with the Emperor Ferdinand, Kossuth, the Hungarian leader, took up an uncompromisingly hostile attitude. Jellacic marched to Pesth. A revolutionary movement of sympathy with Hungary broke out in Vienna. The Emperor fled to Olmutz. Windischgrätz, the Austrian general, marched on Vienna and took possession in November 1848. Ferdinand abdicated, and Francis Joseph, his nephew, became Emperor December 2nd. The Hungarians refused to acknowledge him. There was a rising of Roumanians in Transylvania, and the whole Hungarian nation was called to arms.

Course of the War:

The Austrians occupied Pesth on January 5, 1849; the Hungarians withdrew to Debreczin and were defeated at Kapolona on February 26th. In April the Magyar troops recovered and the Austrians were driven out of Hungary. On April 19th Hungary was proclaimed an independent state. Russia intervened to assist Austria, and marched an army across Galicia. The Hungarians were now confronted with a force three times the size of their own, and the main army capitulated at Vilagos on August 13, 1849.

Political Result:

Hungary was completely crushed and subjected to savage punishment by its conquerors. Every vestige of its old constitutional rights was extinguished.

Remarks:

In 1860 the old Constitution was restored. In 1867 the Emperor Francis Joseph was crowned King of Hungary. A responsible ministry was appointed, and a financial agreement (Ausgleich) made between Austria and Hungary.

Nationality asserted itself in spite of all attempts at repression. But the Hungarians, in their turn, held the Slav and Roumanian populations within their borders with an iron grasp and failed to gain their affection.

THE ITALIAN WAR OF LIBERATION

1831, 1848–1849, 1859 and 1866–1867

Belligerents:

> The States of Italy.
> Austria.
> France.

Cause:

Italy, after the fall of Napoleon, was divided into separate ill-governed small states, with Venice and Lombardy in the hands of Austria. The idea of uniting Italy under one Government grew as the century advanced, and received fresh impetus from the revolutionary movements in Europe in 1830 and 1848. The society, "Young Italy," under the guidance of Mazzini, kept the spirit of revolution alive, although several insurrections instigated by them failed. The expulsion of Austria became the central idea of the movement.

Occasion:

The quarrels between the smaller states: the hatred of the presence of Austria, who, under Metternich's guidance, desired throughout to suppress the movement: the decline of Austrian power on the rise of Prussia: the intervention of France to prevent Austrian aggrandizement and to protect the Pope.

Course of the Wars:

The revolt in the Papal States in 1831 was suppressed by Austrian intervention. France also intervened, and the Austrian troops withdrew. In 1848 Sardinian troops advanced against Austria, but after much fighting round Verona were defeated at Santa Lucia.

Civil war broke out between Naples and Sicily. Sardinia and Piedmont, under Victor Emmanuel and his Minister, Cavour, now took the lead. France became their ally in 1859. In spite of attempts at mediation by Great Britain, Austria presented an ultimatum, April 23, 1859. Napoleon III and the Allies won victories at Magenta and Solferino. By the *Peace of Villa Franca* in July, followed by the *Treaty of Zurich*, November 10, 1859, Austria ceded Lombardy but not Venice.

Tuscany, Parma Modena, and Romagna were united to Piedmont by their own vote. Savoy and Nice were ceded to France.

In 1860 Garibaldi conquered Sicily and Naples. Piedmontese troops entered the Papal States. By 1861 all Italy, with the exception of Rome and Venice, was under Victor Emmanuel. In the North war broke out again. The Italians were defeated by Austria at Custozza, but after Königgrätz (see p. 50) the Austrians ceded Venice to France, and Napoleon III handed it over to Italy. This arrangement was confirmed by the *Treaty of Vienna*, October 3, 1866, between Austria and Italy. In 1867 France defended the Papal States against Garibaldi's invasion, and he was defeated at Mentana. Finally, in 1870, Napoleon III withdrew his troops from Papal territory, and on September 20th Victor Emmanuel entered Rome.

Political Result:

All Italy became united under one monarch with its capital at Rome. Victor Emmanuel was succeeded in 1878 by Humbert, the father of King Victor Emmanuel III.

Remarks:

The rivalry between Austria and Italy did not die down, and there were still certain territories—*Italia irredenta* (such as Trentino)—which remained in Austrian hands.

THE CRIMEAN WAR

1854–1856

Belligerents:

Great Britain, France, Turkey and Sardinia.
Russia.

Cause:

From 1830 onwards there was a growing estrangement between Great Britain and Russia. The Czar Nicholas believed that the dominion of the Turk in Europe was nearing its end, and cherished the ambition that Russia should acquire provinces of the Ottoman dominions. On the other hand, there was keen opposition in Great Britain to Russia's expansion, and to the idea of Constantinople falling into her hands. Louis Napoleon had only two years previously become Emperor of the French. His dynastic ambitions made him eager for military glory. Sardinia joined the Allies for tactical reasons.

Occasion:

The French claimed the custody of the Holy Places in Palestine: the Russians made a counter-claim to the custody of the Holy Places and to a Protectorate over the Greek Christians in the Ottoman Empire. The Turkish Government, on the advice of the British Ambassador, Lord Stratford de Redcliffe, refused to accept the Russian claims. Russian troops crossed the Pruth in June 1853, and a Turkish squadron was destroyed at Sinope in November. On the refusal of Russia to make her ships re-enter port in the Black Sea and evacuate the Danubian principalities, war was declared by France and England on March 27, 1854.

Course of the War:

The Crimea was invaded, and fighting continued there for two years. The Austrian attempt at mediation in May 1855, failed. The Russians were defeated at Alma and Inkerman, and Sevastopol, after a long siege, fell on September 9, 1855. The Russians captured Kars in November.

Political Results:

By the *Treaty of Paris*, March 30, 1856, the Black Sea was neutralized. An engagement was made by all the Powers to respect the independence and integrity of the Ottoman Empire: the Sultan promised to give equality of treatment to his Christian subjects. The Danubian provinces were granted independence under the sovereignty of the Sultan.

Remarks:

This treaty was absolutely barren. The Sultan's promise was never acted on: the neutrality of the Black Sea was maintained only till 1870: and when the integrity of the Ottoman Empire was assailed in later years none of the signatory Powers intervened in its defence. But at the Congress of Berlin in 1878 the Powers partitioned parts of the Ottoman Empire. So far from settling any disputes this war caused dissensions which led to other wars.

THE INDIAN MUTINY

1857–1858

Belligerents:

Great Britain.
Native Indians.

Cause:

The East India Company had engaged in constant wars and employed an army in which native troops outnumbered the British by eight to one. The Sepoys especially became aware of their strength and importance. In many ways religious sensibilities were offended, dissatisfaction with the Company's rule spread and unrest was abroad.

Occasion:

The spirit of revolt grew, and a trivial incident was sufficient to make the spark burst into a flame. Cartridges used for the new Enfield rifle smeared with the fat of sacred cows and the lard of polluted pigs were to be bitten by Hindu and Mohammedan alike. The ferment caused by the rumour spread and the mutiny broke out.

Course of the War:

Native troops mutinied at Mirat, and proceeded to Delhi, Cawnpore, and Lucknow. Many British men and women were murdered. A British force in June and July 1857 marched on Delhi. Engagements were fought, in which there were heavy losses. Disease and cholera also carried off many victims. After a great struggle Lahore was captured in September, and Agra was relieved, also Cawnpore, where, under Nana Sahib, the most hideous massacres and cruelty had taken place. At Lucknow a heroic resistance was made against an overwhelming force of rebels. It was relieved on November 22, 1857. In March 1858, the whole province of Oudh was recovered by Outram and Colin Campbell. Not till the beginning of 1859 did organized resistance come to an end in all parts of India.

Political Result:

By the Queen's proclamation of November 1858 the government of India was taken over by the British Government. The Queen declared that all her Indian subjects should be protected in the exercise of their religious observances. Excessive measures of repression which had been resorted to were stopped.

Remarks:

Queen Victoria was styled Empress of India at the instance of Disraeli in 1876. Various reforms have been instituted in Indian administration tentatively allowing Indians some share in the government of the country. But the problem of British rule in India is not one which is capable of final solution.

THE CHINESE WAR

1857–1860

Belligerents:

Great Britain, France.
China.

Cause:

The increasing commercial ambitions of Western Powers in the East led Great Britain and France to insist on the establishment of fair and equitable terms of trade. The Chinese Government was in the hands of the Tatars known as the Taipings, who, by their successful rebellion, had overthrown the Manchu dynasty.

Occasion:

The refusal of the Chinese Government to redress long-standing grievances or to allow the diplomatic representatives of the Western Powers to reside in Peking; the seizure of the crew of the British ship *Arrow* off Canton, and the refusal of the Chinese Governor to apologize or surrender the men, and the murder of a French missionary in Kwangsi brought things to a head.

Course of the War:

Canton was taken by the British in December 1857. The Taku Forts fell in May 1858 and Tientsin was occupied. Negotiations were attempted but failed. An allied force of British and French landed in 1860, marched on Peking, and the Chinese yielded.

Political Result:

By the treaty of October 24, 1860, the Chinese paid an indemnity of eight million taels. The right of Europeans to travel in the interior was granted, and freedom guaranteed to the preaching of Christianity. By the customs tariff agreed upon the import of opium was legalized. In the course of 1861 British, French, and Russian legations were permanently established at Peking, and in the following years the same right was conceded to other European nations. By treaties with Russia in the same year China ceded all its territory north of the Amur to Russia, and in this territory Vladivostock was founded.

Good relations having been established, the Chinese Government, with the assistance of Gordon, carried out a successful campaign against the Taipings, and the Manchu dynasty was restored.

Remarks:

This was the opening of the door into China, and from henceforth the Western Powers began to compete for commercial and territorial prizes in the Chinese Empire.

AMERICAN CIVIL WAR

1861–1865

Belligerents:

The Northern states of North America.
The Southern states of North America.

Cause:

The cultivation of cotton progressed under very different conditions in the North and South. In the North the white man had to work vigorously to overcome the disadvantages of the soil. In the South the negrolabourer could be used with profit to his owner, and was held as a slave. By 1860 the thirteen original states were enlarged to thirty-three. The territories of the North-east found their prosperity in free labour, the South throve on the cotton crop and continued to exploit negrolabour. The Southern states gradually combined together, and between 1830 and 1850 gained a predominant voice in the control of Federal affairs. The North also became consolidated, and a strong movement against slavery grew up, chiefly owing to the efforts of W. Lloyd Garrison. A new Republican party gained strength in its opposition to the dominating differences of the South, and sectional political differences were intensified. The prospect of the abolition of slavery was not the only issue. The South resented the idea that coercive measures might be used to keep the lower South in the Union. They believed this to be an attack on the doctrine of the sovereignty of states. A widespread feeling in favour of secession grew up.

Occasion:

The Republican party triumphed at the election, and Abraham Lincoln became President in November, 1860. South Carolina seceded, ten other states followed, and the Confederate States were established under the Presidency of Jefferson Davis. The attack on Fort Sumter by the Confederates on April 4, 1861, made war inevitable.

Course of the War:

The North was defeated at Bull Run in July 1861, but captured forts Henry and Donelson in 1862, and gained a victory at Shiloh. At

Richmond, and later at Fredericksburg, the North was defeated. Lincoln issued his proclamation of Emancipation on January 1, 1863. The South, under Lee, were defeated in the greatest battle of the war at Gettysburg, on July 4th. In 1864 there were further victories for the North under Grant at Spottsylvania and Coldharbour; and Atlanta and Savanah were captured. In 1865 Petersburg and Richmond were evacuated by the Confederates and Lee surrendered. On May 26th the war came to an end, after a desperate struggle of nearly four years.

Political Result:

The Union was restored and slavery abolished. Lincoln was assassinated on April 14, 1865, and his wise counsel was lost therefore for the difficult work of reconstruction which followed the war.

Remarks:

Great Britain declared neutrality at the outset, and thereby implicitly, though not explicitly, recognized the Southern Confederacy as a belligerent Power. There was much sympathy with the South among the governing class, but the people were on the side of the North. The Trent affair brought Great Britain and America very near to war. (See *Treaty of Washington*, p. 94.)

FRENCH EXPEDITION IN MEXICO

1862–1867

Belligerents:

France.
Mexican Republicans.

Cause:

From 1789, the date of the first conspiracy against Spain, down to 1857, when a Constitution was promulgated, Mexico was in a state of permanent warfare. In 1861 France, Spain, and Great Britain adopted joint measures against the republic in order to get better protection for their subjects and their property. In 1862 Great Britain and Spain withdrew. But Napoleon III conceived the project of establishing a monarchy in Mexico under his patronage, and so increasing French ascendancy beyond the Atlantic.

Occasion:

The financial misdemeanours of the Mexican Government were made the pretext for the advance of French troops into Mexico in 1862.

Course of the War:

The French force was checked in May 1862, and further reinforcements were sent out. They advanced again in February 1863, and entered Mexico City in June. A Provisional Government was established, and the crown was offered to Maximilian of Austria, who accepted it and reached Mexico City in June 1864. Juarez, the republican leader, was driven into the extreme north of the country. But his resistance was by no means overcome. Napoleon III bound himself to keep a force in Mexico for the protection of Maximilian. In 1865, on the restoration of peace after the Civil War in the United States, the Government of Washington refused to acknowledge any authority in Mexico but that of Juarez. The French were obliged to withdraw in 1867, and Maximilian was left to his fate. The Juarists got the upper hand, and Maximilian was executed.

Political Result:

Juarez, as President of Mexico, was succeeded by Diaz in 1877; and order was maintained for a generation.

Remarks:

This foolish enterprise damaged the reputation of Napoleon III. He was regarded as a political adventurer, and became increasingly unpopular in his own country.

BRAZILIAN WAR

1864–1870

Belligerents:

Brazil, Uruguay, Argentine Republic.
Paraguay.

Cause:

Brazil was part of the Portuguese possessions until 1822, when it declared its independence. The Emperors Pedro I and II had frequent trouble not only with the republican movement in Brazil itself, but with the neighbouring states, with whom they were constantly at war. In 1855 Pedro II sent a squadron up the Parana to adjust several questions outstanding with the republic of Paraguay. Although certain rights were granted to Brazil the Government of Paraguay threw every obstacle in the way to prevent a settlement.

Occasion:

In 1864 Lopez, the ambitious dictator of Paraguay, without declaring war, captured a Brazilian vessel, and invaded Brazil and the Argentine. Uruguay joined them in a triple alliance of defence against Paraguay.

Course of the War:

Owing to the strong natural position of Paraguay, and the obstinacy of Lopez, the war was drawn out with constant fighting and great sacrifice of life in addition to vast expenditure, until 1870, when it was terminated by the capture and death of Lopez.

Political Result:

External troubles ceased, but the republican movement gained in strength until 1889, when Pedro was deposed and a republic declared in Brazil.

Remarks:

The slaughter in this war was so terrific that the population of Paraguay was reduced from 1,337,439 to 221,079.

This is only one example of the very frequent disturbances, both internal and external, in the South American continent during the course of the century.

THE DANISH WAR

1864

Belligerents:

> Denmark.
> Prussia and Austria.

Cause:

The strong revival of nationalism in Germany after the Napoleonic Wars spread to the German inhabitants of the Duchies of Schleswig Holstein, who desired in 1848 to be incorporated as a single constitutional state in the German Federation. The Danish crown could be inherited by female heirs, but in the Duchies the Salic law had never been repealed. This made complications with regard to the succession. Frederick VII of Denmark endeavoured to preserve the Duchy as an integral part of Denmark. An insurrection broke out, and Prussia intervened by marching troops into Holstein. Under pressure from other Powers the King of Prussia signed a convention at Malmoe practically yielding all the Danish demands, and in 1850, by the *Treaty of Berlin*, peace was restored between Prussia and Denmark, but without any settlement of the vexed question. In 1852 Great Britain intervened with a proposal without success. In 1854 the King of Denmark promulgated special Constitutions for the Duchies as well as a common Constitution for the whole Monarchy. The German Confederation rejected this as the Diets of the Duchies had not been consulted. The question became of European interest: its complexity prevented any settlement being reached. Bismarck alone was quite determined on eventual annexation, and Denmark was equally determined not to yield.

Occasion:

After further diplomatic disputes Austrian and Prussian troops entered Schleswig in February 1864.

Course of the War:

The allied troops broke through the frontier fortifications and occupied the greater part of the Danish mainland. The Danes were overthrown in the island of Alsen, and the German flag carried to the northern extremity of Denmark. A conference was opened in

London, April 1864, but the negotiations broke down and the war continued.

Political Result:

Eventually, by the *Treaty of Vienna*, October 30, 1864, the King of Denmark ceded the rights in the whole of Schleswig Holstein to the Sovereigns of Austria and Prussia jointly.

Remarks:

This was more a diplomatic war than a military war. The conflict was between retention and annexation, and little regard was paid on any side to the desires of the inhabitants of the disputed territory. Although by the *Treaty of London* of 1852 the Powers, including Great Britain, had acknowledged as permanent the principle of the integrity of the Danish Monarchy no steps were taken by them to maintain that principle. The settlement did nothing to prevent the outbreak of war between Prussia and Austria two years later, when Schleswig Holstein was again one of the bones of contention.

THE AUSTRO-PRUSSIAN WAR

1866

Belligerents:

Prussia and some of the smaller North German States and Italy. Austria and the other German States.

Cause:

From 1848 onwards in all the projects for a united Germany there was keen rivalry between Prussia and Austria. Each resisted the domination of the other in any new Empire, and the South German states were inclined to side with Austria against Prussian supremacy. This state of affairs prevented any final scheme from being agreed to. At the same time there were serious differences between Austria and Italy, who was Prussia's ally. Bismarck made up his mind that Austria must be expelled by force of arms from the German Federation. He was an ardent supporter of the House of Hohenzollern.

Occasion:

Austria supported Schleswig Holstein in their struggle for independence against Prussia after the conclusion of the Danish War. An attempted congress of neutrals failed. Austria called on the Diet of Frankfort to take the affairs of Schleswig Holstein into its own hands, and demanded and obtained the mobilization of the whole Federal armies. Prussia declared that this action made an end of the Federal Union, and submitted a new plan for the organization of Germany, which was refused. Diplomatic relations were broken off June 12, 1866.

Course of the War:

Hanover and Hesse Cassel were conquered by Prussia, the Austrians were defeated at Königgrätz, July 3, 1866, and the Prussians pushed forward in sight of Vienna. The Austrians defeated the Italians on land at Custozza, and by sea at Lissa.

Political Result:

Napoleon III offered mediation, which was accepted. The *Treaty of Prague*, August 23, 1866. Prussia annexed Hanover, Nassau, Hesse Cassel, and Frankfort: Germany north of the Main together with

Saxony was included in a Federation under Prussia: the Southern states were left independent. Prussian sovereignty over Schleswig Holstein was recognized. Austria withdrew completely from German affairs.

Remarks:

Napoleon III had attempted, by dividing Germany in two, to put an obstacle in the way of German unity. His clumsy diplomacy was greatly disapproved of in France. By preventing a final settlement he made the recurrence of war inevitable.

BRITISH EXPEDITION IN ABYSSINIA

1867–1868

Belligerents:

Great Britain.
Abyssinia.

Cause:

From 1855 Abyssinia came under the powerful rule of the Emperor Theodore. He subdued the neighbouring kingdoms of Tigré and Shoa, and took Menelek, son of the ruler of Tigré, to be trained in his service. He ravaged the surrounding country, and oppressed his own people. In 1864 there was an interchange of letters between Theodore and the British Government, out of which difficulties arose.

Occasion:

The British Consul and his staff, and subsequently a British emissary, were imprisoned in Magdala and put in chains. Their release was demanded, but the Emperor paid no attention, and the British Government decided they must have recourse to arms.

Course of the War:

A British force under Sir Robert Napier landed in January 1868, a march of three hundred miles was undertaken through the mountainous districts, and, after a fierce engagement, Magdala was stormed and taken on April 13, 1868. The Emperor committed suicide, and his son was taken to England, where he died. The British troops left the country in May 1868.

Political Result:

The ruler of Tigré succeeded Theodore under the title of King John, and on his death, in 1889, Menelek became Emperor.

Remarks:

After this the Italians came on to the scene with ambitions in this part of Africa (see p. 74), but Abyssinia remained an independent kingdom. In the various expeditions against the Mullah in Somaliland (1902–4) the Abyssinians co-operated with Great Britain.

THE FRANCO-GERMAN WAR

1870–1871

Belligerents:

France.
Prussia and ten other German States.

Cause:

For some years previously there had been increasing friction between France and Prussia, owing chiefly to Louis Napoleon's apprehensions as to the possibility of closer union between Prussia and the South German states, his repeated endeavours to extend the Eastern frontier of France, and Bismarck's counter-moves to frustrate his designs. The desire also for a united Germany was growing stronger, and Bismarck believed it could not be completed without a conflict with France.

Occasion:

The candidature of Prince Leopold of Hohenzollern Sigmaringen for the throne of Spain in 1870 was resented by France as calculated to bring Spain under the influence of Prussia. King William of Prussia, on representations from France, persuaded Prince Leopold to withdraw, but refused firmly but politely a guarantee against the renewal of the candidature. Bismarck published a telegram conveying the impression that the French Ambassador, Benedetti, had been insulted by the King at Ems on the occasion of the refusal. This infuriated public opinion in France, the Empress Eugénie actively used her influence, and Napoleon agreed to a declaration of war on July 14, 1870.

Course of the War:

In the war, which lasted from July 1870 to February 1871, the ill-organized and badly led French troops could make no stand against the well-prepared armies of Germany. The French were defeated at Wörth, August 6th; Metz, August 7th; Marsla Tour, August 17th; Gravelotte, August 18th. Paris was besieged: Louis Napoleon capitulated at Sedan, September 2nd; Strasburg fell, September 28th; Bazaine capitulated at Metz, October 27th; and the Germans entered Paris on January 28, 1871.

Political Result:

By the *Treaty of Frankfort*, May 10, 1871, Alsace and half Lorraine (with Metz) were ceded to Germany, and an indemnity of 200 millions was exacted from France. The King of Prussia was proclaimed at Versailles German Emperor. France was declared a republic, and Napoleon eventually retired into exile in England.

Remarks:

The dictation of terms and the annexation of Alsace-Lorraine entirely prevented friendly relations from being established between the two countries in the succeeding years. France, by getting rid of the corrupt and incompetent government of Napoleon III, began to recuperate from this time onward. Germany, having reached the ideal of unity, proceeded gradually to join in the competition for commercial expansion and Imperial aggrandizement.

THE ASHANTI WAR

1873–1874

Belligerents:

> Great Britain.
> The Ashantis.

Cause:

The Ashantis, a very fierce and warlike tribe on the Gold Coast of Africa had repeatedly caused trouble owing to their treatment of the Fantis, a tribe on the coast under British protection. In 1824 they defeated a British force and carried off to Kumasi the skull of the Governor, Sir Charles M'Carthy, which was used as a royal drinking cup. They were afterwards defeated in 1826. In 1863 an expedition against them had to be abandoned owing to the ravages done by sickness among the troops. In 1867 a warlike king, Kofi Karikari succeeded as ruler and proceeded to make hostile preparations against the Fantis.

Occasion:

In 1872 some Dutch possessions on the Gold Coast were transferred to Great Britain. The King of Ashanti claimed a tribute formerly allowed to him by the Dutch and refused to evacuate the territory ceded to Britain. He also held four Europeans in captivity. The British Government determined to take up the matter seriously, and when in January 1873 an Ashanti force invaded the British Protectorate an expedition under Sir Garnet Wolseley was immediately despatched.

Course of the War:

Owing to difficulties of climate it was necessary that the whole campaign should be rapidly carried out. The Ashantis were defeated at all points. Kumasi was reached and King Kofi surrendered. The European troops suffered severely from fever but the objects were successfully accomplished. Wolseley sailed from England on September 12, 1873, and returned to Portsmouth on March 21, 1874.

Political Result:

The King renounced his claim to supremacy over any part of the former Dutch protectorate, paid an indemnity in gold, and agreed to prohibit human sacrifices. Further trouble arose, however, after the death of the King, his successors disregarding the treaty. In 1895 an expedition was sent out under Colonel Sir F. Scott. Kumasi was occupied and King Prempeh deported. Still the Ashanti tribes refused to submit, and continued in rebellion. The Governor of the Gold Coast and a small force were surrounded in Kumasi. He managed to escape and Kumasi was finally relieved by an expedition under Colonel Wilcocks who gradually suppressed the rebellion. By an Order in Council of September 26, 1901, Ashanti was formally annexed to the British dominions and given a separate administration under the control of the Governor of the Gold Coast.

Remarks:

Imperial responsibilities entail the protection of friendly tribes against hostile attack in the outlying parts of the Empire. Punitive expeditions become necessary and annexation is found to be the best method of securing law and order.

RUSSO-TURKISH WAR

1877–1878

Belligerents:

> Russia.
> Turkey.

Cause:

The persecution and oppression of Christians in the Ottoman Empire led to a revolt in Herzegovina in 1875. Andrassy, on behalf of Austria, presented a Note to the Turkish Government demanding reforms, and this was followed by the Berlin Memorandum, signed by Germany, France, Austria, Russia, and Italy. Great Britain alone stood out. The Bulgarian massacres in June 1876 caused a great sensation in England, and were followed by a declaration of war by Servia and Montenegro against Turkey. Great Britain, always mistrusting Russian designs, called a Conference. The demands of the Conference were rejected by Turkey in January 1877. The Sultan protested against the encroachment of the Powers on his inviolable rights.

Occasion:

The London Protocol of March 1877, signed by Great Britain and Russia and agreed to by the other Powers, called for reforms and expressed the intention of the Powers to safeguard the Christian population. This was also rejected by the Turks, and Russia declared war on April 24, 1877.

Course of the War:

The Russian army crossed the Danube. Plevna fell in December 1877. The Russians entered Adrianople, January 1878. The advance of the Russian army towards Gallipoli was followed by the dispatch of the British fleet to Constantinople and brought Russia and Great Britain within a hair's-breadth of war. This, however, was avoided and peace negotiations began.

Political Result:

Treaty of San Stefano, March 3, 1878. The independence of Servia, Montenegro, and Roumania was recognized. Bulgaria was made an autonomous principality with frontiers including the greater part of European Turkey; the Dobrudja and certain districts in Asia Minor were ceded to Russia.

Great Britain objected strongly to this treaty, and proposed a Congress at Berlin. While the chances of the Congress hung in the balance, Great Britain made warlike preparations, but the Congress was finally agreed to.

Treaty of Berlin, July 13, 1878. Bulgaria's frontier was confined to the country north of the Balkans. Bosnia and Herzegovina were handed over to Austria: the territory given to Serbia and Montenegro was further restricted: Thessaly and part of Epirus were ceded to Greece.

By a secret convention Great Britain engaged to protect Turkey against further aggression of Russia in Asia. In return the Porte assigned Cyprus to be occupied and administered by England.

Lord Beaconsfield was the British Plenipotentiary at the Peace Congress and returned declaring he had secured "peace with honour."

Remarks:

This was a patched-up peace. It settled none of the problems in the Balkans, which continued to be the danger zone in Europe for the rest of the century.

THE SECOND AFGHAN WAR

1878–1881

Belligerents:

Great Britain and Indian Troops.
Afghanistan.

Cause:

In 1868 the expanding power of Russia in Asia resulted in Bokhara becoming a Russian dependency. In 1873 Russia conquered Khiva. Shere Ali, now ruler of Afghanistan, became alarmed, but failing to come to an understanding with the British Government, he began to make overtures to Russia. In 1877 an offer of alliance was made by the Viceroy of India, but Shere Ali refused to admit a British Agent into Afghanistan.

Occasion:

In 1878 the Russian Government sent an envoy to Kabul to make a treaty with the Amir. A British army was also sent, but was turned back on the frontier, and hostilities were proclaimed by the Viceroy.

Course of the War:

Two British forces marched into the interior of Afghanistan, and occupied important positions. Shere Ali fled from his capital, and died in February 1879. By the *Treaty of Gandamuk*, May 1879, Yakub Khan was recognized as Amir, and he agreed that a British envoy should reside at his Court. In September 1879, the envoy, his staff, and his escort were massacred. A fresh expedition was sent under Sir F. Roberts, who entered Kabul. In 1880, Abdur Rahman, nephew of Shere Ali, returned from exile in Russia and established himself in the northern provinces. The British Government came to an agreement with him, and he was recognized as Amir. In July 1880 Ayub Khan, another son of Shere Ali, defeated a British force at Maiwand. Roberts reached Kandahar from Kabul by a rapid march, and defeated Ayub Khan on September 1, 1880. Again, in July 1881, Ayub Khan returned and took possession of Kandahar, but was finally routed by Abdur Rahman in September.

Political Result:

The frontiers of Afghanistan were delimited in agreement with Russia. Abdur Rahman's rulership over Afghanistan was established. He extended and consolidated his dominion over the whole country, and was peacefully succeeded by his son Habibullah in 1901.

Remarks:

By the Anglo-Russia Convention of 1907, Great Britain engaged not to alter the political status of Afghanistan, and Russia recognized it as outside her sphere of influence.

THE ZULU WAR

1879

Belligerents:

> Great Britain.
> The Zulus.

Cause:

The warlike and threatening attitude of the Zulus under Cetywayo constituted a perpetual menace to the safety of the British possessions in South Africa. The policy of Sir Bartle Frere, Governor of the Cape and High Commissioner, was the eventual Federation of all South African states under British rule, and it was essential, therefore, in his opinion, that the white inhabitants should be secured against native raids. There was a strong opinion that this could be effected without force of arms.

Occasion:

The cruelties and excesses practised by Cetywayo culminated in a raid into Natal, where women were carried off and murdered. Frere issued an ultimatum demanding the break-up of the military system of Zululand, and further that a British Resident was to be received and missionaries were not to be molested. No reply was received, and British troops entered Zululand on January 10, 1879.

Course of the War:

Frere's application for reinforcements was refused by the British Government. But after a British defeat at Isandhlwana, January 22, 1879, which was only prevented from being a disaster by the gallant defence of Rorke's Drift, Sir Garnet Wolseley was sent out with more troops. The Zulus were defeated at Ulundi, July 5th, and Cetywayo was taken prisoner.

Political Result:

Zululand was divided into thirteen districts, each with a separate chief, and was placed under a British Resident. It was finally annexed in 1887.

Remarks:

This war is only an episode in the extension and consolidation of the British Empire in South Africa. But it is an instance of the grave responsibilities which are involved in Imperial expansion.

In the course of the war the Prince Imperial, only son of Napoleon III, was killed, and with him died the last hopes of a restoration of the Napoleonic dynasty in France.

THE CHILE-PERUVIAN WAR

1879–1882

Belligerents:

> Chile.
> Peru. Bolivia.

Cause:

After the blockade and bombardment of their ports by a Spanish squadron in 1865, on account of their sympathy with Peru in a quarrel with Spain, the Chileans were impressed with the necessity of possessing an adequate fleet to defend their long coast line. Ships were obtained and officers trained, so that Chile became well equipped for any future encounter.

The authorities of Bolivia seized the effects of the Chilean Nitrate Company at Antofogasta.

Occasion:

Five hundred soldiers were despatched to protect Chilean interests. The force landed and marched inland. Bolivia declared war on March 1st, Peru on April 5, 1879.

Course of the War:

The Chileans occupied every port on the Bolivian coast, and engaged the Peruvian fleet. The *Huascar*, a Peruvian ironclad, after other ships had been destroyed, did great damage under four successive commanders, but after severe fighting was forced to surrender off Angamos, and the Peruvian navy ceased to exist. After several engagements on land the Chileans succeeded in taking possession of the Bolivian seaboard and the Peruvian province of Tarapaca.

Fighting continued in 1880 when, in spite of daring resistance, the Peruvians were defeated at all points. Lima was occupied on January 17, 1881, and Callao surrendered on January 18th. The last engagement took place in September 1882, and a small army of occupation was left in Peru.

Political Result:

The Treaty of Peace was not ratified till April 1884. Peru ceded to Chile the province of Tarapaca. The provinces of Tacna and Arica were placed under Chilean authority for ten years, after which they were to decide their own future government. Chile, however, eventually evaded compliance with this agreement and retained forcible possession of the provinces. Chile retained possession of the Bolivian seaboard, thus cutting off Bolivia from access to the Pacific.

Remarks:

The aggressive attitude of Chile was a cause of complaint with the neighbouring states, and nearly led on more than one occasion to further conflict. By a Treaty signed in 1905, however, Bolivia at last ceded all claims to a seaport and strip of coast. Chile, except for a civil war in 1891, is distinguished among the South American States by its freedom from revolution and serious political unrest.

THE FRENCH EXPEDITION IN TUNIS

1881

Belligerents:

France.
The Arabs of Tunis.

Cause:

Tunis under the government of the Beys formed part of the Ottoman Empire. In 1862 Italy began to take an interest in Tunis. A triple British, French, and Italian control over Tunisian finances was established in 1869. In 1878, at the Congress of Berlin, Great Britain came to a secret understanding to allow France a free hand in Tunis in return for French acquiescence in the British lease of Cyprus.

Occasion:

In 1880 the Italians bought the British railway from Tunis to Golitta. France, under the pretext of chastising independent tribes in the north-east, determined to take action.

Course of the War:

A French force marched on the capital. The conquest of the country was not effected without serious resistance, specially at Sjax, but finally the whole country was brought completely under French jurisdiction, and the Bey was compelled to accept a French protectorate.

Political Result:

By the *Treaty of Bardo*, May 12, 1881, and a further *Treaty of La Marsa*, June 8, 1883, the French protectorate was established. Italy did not recognize the full consequences of the French protectorate till 1896. Protests by Turkey were ignored by France, and in 1892 the Ottoman Government was prepared to delimit the Tunis-Tripoli frontier. But there were various frontier incidents, and Turkey maintained the claim that the Tunisians were Ottoman subjects.

Remarks:

The occupation of Tunis led to an estrangement between France and Italy.

THE EGYPTIAN WAR

1882

Belligerents:

> Great Britain.
> Egypt.

Cause:

> Since 1840, while Egypt had been virtually independent, Great Britain had been regarded as the special champion of Turkish suzerainty; France as the protector of the Viceroys of Egypt. The construction of the Suez Canal, chiefly engineered by France and Great Britain, made Egypt of new importance, as the direct route to India now lay through the Red Sea. An Anglo-French financial control was established to secure payment of interest on the enormous sums lent to the Khedive Ismail. British influence became paramount, and the British Government gradually assumed the responsibility for good government in Egypt.

Occasion:

> An anti-Turkish revolt under Arabi Pasha broke out, and there was a massacre of Christians in Alexandria in June 1882. The Khedive was powerless. The Powers met in conference at Constantinople, but before any decision was arrived at the British Government resolved to act.

Course of the War:

> The bombardment of Alexandria took place on July 11, 1882, and the Egyptian troops set fire to the town. The Sultan was willing to enter into a military convention with Great Britain, but before it was signed the Egyptians were defeated at Tel-el Kebir by the British under Sir Garnet Wolseley, on September 13, 1882, and Arabi surrendered.

Political Result:

> Arabi and other Pashas were banished to Ceylon.

The military occupation of Egypt by Great Britain, in spite of declarations to the effect that the troops would shortly be withdrawn, and in spite of protests from France, became permanent.

Remarks:

Till the Anglo-French agreement of 1904 France adopted a more or less hostile attitude with regard to Egypt. Many administrative and financial reforms were introduced by Sir Evelyn Baring, afterwards Lord Cromer. The government was practically taken out of the hands of the Egyptians, and from time to time there was trouble with a nationalist movement.

FRANCO-CHINESE WAR

1884–1885

Belligerents:

> France.
> China.

Cause:

> France, after 1870, turned its attention more and more to colonial expansion in Africa, and also in Asia, where for some time efforts had been made by the French to indemnify themselves in Indo-China for the loss of Hindustan. In 1875 a vague treaty with the Emperor of Annam gave France the protectorate. The importance was realized of finding a path of penetration towards China.

Occasion:

> In 1883–1884 an attempt was made to force the Emperor of Annam to acknowledge the protectorate and to secure the delta of Tonkin. The Chinese Government, unwilling to have France as a neighbour, took the offensive.

Course of the War:

> The French fleet destroyed the arsenal of Foochow, took possession of Formosa, Kelung, and the Pescadores Islands, and blockaded Southern China. A French brigade was put to flight near Langsen. Incorrect information as to the extent of the reverse caused the overthrow of Jules Ferry's ministry. But the victories and blockade of the French fleet induced China to accept peace.

Political Result:

> By the *Treaty of Tientsin*, June 9, 1885, China recognized the French protectorate in Tonkin and Annam, and promised to open the southern provinces to French traders.

> By treaties with Siam in 1893, and Great Britain in 1892–1896, Cambodia came also under French protection, and the Empire in Indo-China was consolidated.

Remarks:

France definitely joined in the competition for Imperial expansion.

THE BURMESE WARS

1823–1826, 1851, 1885

Belligerents:

> Great Britain.
> Burma.

Cause:

> The expansion of the British Empire in India involved the subjection of neighbouring states. In addition to this there was fear of the rivalry of France in Burma.

Occasions:

> (1) The conquest of Assam, which was under British protection, by the King of Ava in 1823, and the attack by him on a British fort at Shapur, led to the declaration of war against Burma.

> (2) The insults offered to the British flag at Rangoon by the King of Ava, led to the fresh outbreak of war in 1851.

> (3) King Thibaw's despotic rule and his design to enter into an agreement with France, led to the last Ultimatum in 1885.

Course of the Wars:

> (I) A British force was defeated at Ramu, and the first two attempts to reach Ava failed. Martaban and Tennasserin were taken by the British, and the Burmese were expelled from Rangoon in December 1824. Prome was reached in April 1825. Myede was entered in December. In 1826 Sir Archibald Campbell pushed on to Yandabu, forty-five miles from Ava. By the treaty of peace February 24, 1826, the British gained the provinces of Assam, Arakan, and the coast of Tenasserim.

> (II) In April, 1852, as the King of Ava refused to come to terms, Rangoon, Martaban, and Bassein were taken by Dalhousie. Prome was taken in October, and Pegu in November 1852. No treaty was signed but the King was prepared to accept an accomplished fact.

> (III) In 1885 the British Ultimatum took King Thibaw by surprise, and within a fortnight he surrendered unconditionally when the

British force approached his capital. Guerilla warfare continued for nearly two years.

Political Result:

By the proclamation of January 1, 1886, the whole of Burma was annexed, and Thibaw was deported to India.

Remarks:

The conquest of Burma was affected, not so much because of the misrule of the Kings of Ava as from a motive of Imperial expansion and the desire to forestall the designs of France.

THE SERBO-BULGARIAN WAR

1885

Belligerents:

> Bulgaria.
> Serbia.

Cause:

The Treaty of Berlin of 1878 left abundant material for future conflict in European Turkey. Bulgaria was confined to the north of the Balkan mountains, and Eastern Roumelia was still under the Sultan. Prince Alexander of Battenberg, the ruler of Bulgaria, in September 1885, marched south and occupied Philippopolis. The Sultan protested, the Czar was indignant, but Great Britain approved the Union of Roumelia with Bulgaria, and the danger of war passed away. The success of Bulgaria whetted the appetite of Milan, who had become King of Serbia in 1882. With a view to strengthening the prestige of his dynasty he adopted a spirited foreign policy and awaited an opportunity.

Occasion:

Frontier troubles and tariff disputes between the two countries had embittered relations, and the King of Serbia declared war, thinking he would have a triumphal march to Sofia, the Russian officers having withdrawn from the Bulgarian army.

Course of the War:

The Bulgarians gained a decisive victory at Slivnitsa on November 16, 1885, and occupied Pirot, and the road to Belgrade lay open before them. But Austria intervened on behalf of Serbia, and after fourteen days' fighting an armistice was signed.

Political Result:

By the *Treaty of Buckarest*, March 3, 1886, the *status quo* was restored; Bulgaria gained nothing, but established her right to Eastern Roumelia. Owing to Russian intrigue Alexander was forced to abdicate and was succeeded by Ferdinand of Saxe-Coburg as Prince of Bulgaria.

Remarks:

Bulgaria became gradually the most advanced and formidable state in the Balkans. In 1908, at the time of the revolutionary crisis in Turkey and the annexation of Bosnia and Herzogovina by Austria, Ferdinand declared himself Czar of a completely independent Bulgaria.

Milan abdicated in 1889, and his son Alexander became King of Serbia. He and his wife were murdered in 1903 and Peter Karageorgevich accepted the crown.

THE CHINO-JAPANESE WAR

1894–1895

Belligerents:

Japan.
China and Korea.

Cause:

Japan adopting Western ideas developed into a powerful state with surprising rapidity during the last fifty years of the nineteenth century. The growth of her armaments and an ambition for expansion necessarily followed. China, on the other hand, did not welcome the influence of the West, which rapid transit and communication had brought into Asia. The weakness and misgovernment of Korea was a perpetual temptation to her neighbours. Japan invited China to co-operate in demanding reforms in Korea, but China refused and Japan acted alone.

Occasion:

In July 1894 Japan issued an Ultimatum calling on Korea to accept a Japanese programme of reforms. Korea temporized, and Seoul, the capital, was taken without difficulty, the Emperor being made a prisoner. China immediately intervened.

Course of the War:

By land and sea the Japanese, who had been trained by European officers, were easily victorious. Asan was occupied, a victory was gained off the Yalu River, and the Japanese marched on Yingkow. Port Arthur, on the Liao-Tung peninsula, was captured, finally Wei-hai-Wei fell, and Li Hung Chang, the Chinese Minister, sued for peace.

Political Result:

By the *Treaty of Shimonoseki*, China ceded to Japan the Liao Tung peninsula, the island of Formosa and the Pescadores Islands, and the indemnity was fixed at 200 million taels. But Russia, France, and Germany intervened, and ordered Japan to surrender the Liao Tung Peninsula on the ground that Port Arthur threatened the independence of Peking. But the insincerity of the intervention of the

Western Powers was revealed in 1897, when China was compelled to lease Kiao Chow to Germany, Port Arthur to Russia, Wei-hai-Wei to Great Britain, while France obtained a concession near Tonkin. Only the Italian claim for the port of Sanmen was refused by China.

Remarks:

The encroachments of the Western Powers evoked intense indignation in China. The rivalry in the exploitation of the Far East by the West had begun in real earnest.

THE ITALO-ABYSSINIAN WAR

1895–1896

Belligerents:

Italy.
Abyssinia.

Cause:

Having become a united nation, Italy soon developed Imperialistic ambitions. She looked towards Tunis, but was forestalled there by France in 1881. In 1884, being secure from an attack by land, by an alliance with Austria concluded in 1882, and being assured by Great Britain that the occupation by a friendly Power of certain positions on the Red Sea littoral would not be regarded unfavourably, the Italian Government decided on a forward policy in Africa.

Occasion:

After a preliminary expedition in 1887, which was unsuccessful and had to be recalled, a treaty was made with Menelek, after the death of King John of Abyssinia, which was interpreted in Italy as involving Italian suzerainty over Abyssinia. Italy supported Menelek against his rival RasMangascia.

Course of the War:

Italian victories over the Dervishes at Agordat (1893) and Cassala (1894) encouraged the ambition of Italy for a vast African Empire. On a further Italian advance in 1895 the Abyssinians united in their resistance. Menelek repudiated all idea of a protectorate, and General Baratieri suffered a disastrous defeat at Adowah, March 1, 1896.

Political Result:

The Italian suzerainty over Abyssinia was abandoned, and by the Treaty of Peace signed in September 1900, the frontiers of the Italian colony were reduced.

Remarks:

The attempt on the part of Italy to hunt with the lions in colonial aggrandizement ended in humiliation. Italy was now able to devote its attention to much-needed internal reforms. But the Imperialist policy only died down to be revived later.

THE WAR IN THE SOUDAN

1896–1898

Belligerents:

> Great Britain—Egypt.
> Arabs and Dervishes.

Cause:

The Soudan had fallen into the hands of rebellious tribes under the Mahdi. In 1883 on Egyptian force under General Hicks had been defeated at El Obeid, and General Baker was also defeated in his attempt to relieve the Tokar garrison. The successes of a British force near Suakin were rendered useless by the refusal of the British Government to advance further. Early in 1884 it was decided to despatch General Gordon, who had an intimate knowledge of the country, to bring away Europeans from the Soudan. On arriving at Khartoum he was cut off from all communication with Egypt, Berber and the Bahr-el-Gazal province having fallen into the hands of the Mahdi. The relief expedition was sent out too late to save him. Khartoum fell, and Gordon was killed on January 25, 1885. The whole of the Soudan remained under the rule of the Mahdi for thirteen years. The British Government came to the conclusion that Egypt could never be considered permanently secure so long as a hostile Power was in occupation of Khartoum.

Occasion:

After the Italian defeat at Adowah it was decided to create a diversion in Italian interests, and orders were given to occupy the province of Dongola. Rumours of the crumbling power of the Khalifa, who had succeeded the Mahdi, strengthened the idea that it was a favourable opportunity to advance into the Soudan.

Course of the War:

British and Egyptian troops under Kitchener occupied Dongola September 23, 1896. In 1897 desert railways were constructed, and Abu Hamed and Berber were wrested from the dervishes. In 1898 reinforcements of British troops were sent from Cairo. Omdurman, the stronghold of Mahdism, was captured on September 2, 1898, and two days later Khartoum was occupied.

Political Result:

By an agreement between the British and Egyptian Governments in January 1899, the Soudan was placed under their joint control, the Governor-General to be appointed by the Khedive on British recommendation.

Remarks:

The arrival of Major Marchand at Fashoda, in September 1898, where he hoisted the French flag, created a momentary excitement and talk of war, but the British Government adopted a firm attitude, and he received orders to withdraw.

No opposition to the Anglo-Egyptian agreement was encountered in Europe. The economic and agricultural development of the Soudan has since progressed rapidly.

Nearly a million square miles were added to the territory under British rule.

THE TURKO-GREEK WAR

1897

Belligerents:

> Turkey.
> Greece.

Cause:

Crete, which formed part of the Ottoman Dominion, had been granted a Constitution in 1868. A revolt in 1889 caused the Sultan to limit the powers of the assembly and supersede the Christian governor by a Mussulman. Disturbances broke out between Christians and Mohammedans in the succeeding years. In February 1897 the Christians proclaimed union with Greece, and Colonel Vassos was sent with a force to occupy the island in the King's name. The Powers intervened, and the Admirals occupied Canea. Neither the Sultan nor the King wanted war. The King was under the impression that the Powers would prevent it.

Occasion:

Enthusiasm for war which was not accompanied by any sort of military organization or preparation grew up in Greece. When armed bands crossed the frontier into Macedonia, Turkey immediately declared war (April 17, 1897).

Course of the War:

The Greek fleet, on which great hopes had been placed, effected nothing. The Turkish forces occupied Larissa, advanced across Thessaly, defeated the Greeks all along the line, and on May 17, 1897, the victory of Domokos opened to the Turks the pass which leads down to Lamia. The Powers intervened, and a armistice was signed.

Political Result:

By the treaty of peace signed at Constantinople, December 4, 1897, the Turks evacuated Thessaly, and certain strategic alterations were made in the frontier. Greece paid an indemnity of four millions, and accepted the European control of her finances. Crete continued to be the arena of periodic conflict. Prince George of Greece was appointed High Commissioner of the Powers under a new

Constitution, but he resigned in 1906. While virtually Greek the island remained under the suzerainty of the Sultan.

Remarks:

This was only one of the many Balkan conflicts. The intervention of the Powers was invoked in order to check any increase in the dominion of the Sultan. But owing to their own conflicting ambitions and the inherent racial complications in the Balkans, they never at any time reached a solution of the problems involved.

THE SPANISH-AMERICAN WAR

1897–1898

Belligerents:

Spain.
The United States of America.

Cause:

The decline of the Spanish Colonial Empire (which had reached its highest point under Philip II at the end of the sixteenth century) continued throughout the seventeenth, eighteenth, and early nineteenth century, and was hastened by the misgovernment, corruption, and incessant outbreaks of revolution in Spain itself. One by one by means of revolution, the Spanish-American colonies had gained their independence. The policy of the Holy Alliance and of Metternich was to check the growth of Constitutional government in Europe. King Ferdinand of Spain was in conflict with the constitutional movement, and civil war prevailed. In 1823 France intervened in Spain on behalf of Ferdinand, and French troops entered Madrid. Canning, on behalf of Great Britain, prohibited the conquest by France or her allies of the Spanish colonies, and formally recognized their independence in 1824. Cuba and other islands were the last of the Spanish possessions. During the remainder of the nineteenth century Spain continued periodically to be torn and weakened by internal disturbances.

Occasion:

In order to quell the revolts in Cuba more effectually the milder policy of Martinez Campos was exchanged in 1897 for the ruthless and brutal rule of General Weyler. The United States were deeply stirred by the torture and starvation of their neighbours. General Weyler was recalled. But when the American cruiser *Maine* was blown up in the port of Havana, the United States demanded the evacuation of Cuba by Spain. Spain refused.

Course of the War:

Two Spanish fleets were destroyed in May and July 1898, and American land forces in Cuba, the Philippines, and Porto Rico won those islands with comparatively little struggle.

Political Result:

By the treaty of peace signed at Paris, December 1898, Spain surrendered practically all her colonies. The Caroline Islands in the Pacific were sold to Germany in 1899.

Remarks:

This was the last chapter in the extinction of a vast colonial Empire, which was dissolved owing to the spirit of independence in its various states and the bad government in the Mother Country.

THE BOER WAR

1881, 1899–1902

Belligerents:

Great Britain.
The Transvaal and Orange Free State.

Cause:

The premature annexation of the Transvaal in 1877 was resented by the majority of the Boers. In 1880 a formidable rebellion broke out, a small British force was sent out which met with determined opposition at Laing's Nek and Ingogo, and on February 27, 1881, was defeated at Majuba Hill. The Boers regained their independence under the suzerainty of Great Britain.

Cecil Rhodes, with vast ideas of Imperial expansion, became the dominating influence in South Africa. In 1884 Bechuanaland was annexed. In 1889 Rhodes founded the British South Africa Company. In 1896, after a successful conflict with the Matabeles, Buluwayo was captured and Matabeleland added to the territory of Rhodesia. In 1886 gold had been discovered in the Transvaal, and a great cosmopolitan city arose at Johannesburg. This resulted in an enormous influx of Europeans and the decision of the Boers to exclude them from any share in the political life of the country. Behind Rhodes, who became Prime Minister of Cape Colony in 1895, great financial interests grew up and exerted considerable influence. Under the presidency of Kruger the Boers adopted a more and more hostile attitude towards the Outlanders. In 1895 the Jameson Raid, which was connived at by the authorities, revived Kruger's power, which had been waning, and made the Boers arm in preparation for a further surprise.

Occasion:

A promise of intervention was sent by the British Government in reply to a petition from the Outlanders in 1899. Attempts to reach a compromise with Kruger failed. Both sides were preparing for war, and the mining interests exerted great pressure. On October 9, 1899, the Transvaal issued an Ultimatum.

Course of the War:

The Boers invaded Natal and Cape Colony; Ladysmith, Mafeking, and Kimberley were invested. British defeats at Magersfontein, Stormberg, and Colenso (December 1899) led to Lord Roberts being sent out to supersede General Buller. Kimberley and Ladysmith were relieved, Bloemfontein fell. In May 1900 Mafeking was relieved, and in June Johannesburg and Pretoria were occupied. The attempt to insist on unconditional surrender prolonged the war for two more years.

Political Result:

By the *Treaty of Vereeniging*, May 1902, the Transvaal lost its independence. The Orange Free State had been annexed in 1900. Under pressure from the financial interests Chinese were introduced to work the gold-mines. This was one of the chief reasons for the fall of the Conservative Government in 1906. Campbell-Bannerman, who became Prime Minister, solved the problem of the future of the Transvaal by granting them full self-government, and the importation of Chinese was stopped.

Remarks:

The origin of the war can be directly traced to far less worthy causes than that of redressing the grievances of the Outlanders. The war was unnecessarily prolonged by an underestimate of the strength of the Boers and the desire to humiliate them. But the grant of self-government was the act that saved the war from being barren in results and from being the precursor of further trouble. The Union of South Africa was established in 1909.

The Powers of Europe, with the exception of Italy, adopted an unfriendly attitude towards Great Britain during the war.

THE BOXER RISING IN CHINA

1899–1900

Belligerents:

Great Britain, Russia, Germany, France, and Japan.
China.

Cause:

The humiliating results of the war of 1894–5 (p. 72) killed the reform movement in China and brought the reactionary party, headed by the Dowager-Empress, back to power. A society called the Boxers spread very rapidly through the provinces, preaching death to foreigners and receiving official support.

Occasion:

Attacks on Europeans began in 1899, and became very frequent in the early months of 1900. In May the Ministers at Peking asked for additional guards. The Boxers surrounded the city, and Admiral Seymour's attempt to reach the capital was frustrated. The destruction of the Taku Fort by the Allies was treated as a declaration of war, and Chinese Imperial troops joined the Boxers.

Course of the War:

The settlements at Tientsin were rescued by a Russian force. An allied force made its way through from Taku, and forced an entry into Pekin. In August a relief column of 18,000 allied troops defeated the Chinese in several engagements and marched on Pekin. The legations had for eight weeks withstood a siege. The Chinese Government gave foreigners twenty-four hours to leave the capital. The German Minister was murdered in the street. The British Legation formed the refuge of all those who were driven out of their places of retreat. When the relieving force arrived the Chinese only made a faint-hearted defence. The Empress fled, the legations were relieved, and Pekin was occupied.

Political Result:

By the peace protocol, which was signed on September 7, 1901, the punishment of the ringleaders was demanded: the forts between Pekin and the sea were dismantled, permanent guards for the legations were established, and a large indemnity was fixed.

Remarks:

Official intercourse with the Chinese Government was established on a more satisfactory basis. But serious trouble in the Far East and internal disturbances in China itself continued.

THE RUSSO-JAPANESE WAR

1904–1905

Belligerents:

> Russia.
> Japan.

Cause:

When Port Arthur, which Japan had been forced to surrender in 1895, was seized by Russia there was deep indignation in Japan. In 1902 a treaty of alliance was concluded between Great Britain and Japan. Russia undertook to evacuate Manchuria, and although the withdrawal of troops began in 1903, instead of continuing the evacuation Russia demanded new concessions. In Korea Russian speculators obtained concessions, and influential members of the Russian Court were interested in the enterprise. Japan protested.

Occasion:

A treaty regulating the position in Manchuria and Korea was suggested by Japan, but Russia refused to recognize Japan's paramount influence in Korea, and after several months of fruitless negotiation Japan issued an Ultimatum in February 1904.

Course of the War:

After successful initial encounters on the part of Japan, Port Arthur was surrendered on January 1, 1905. After a Japanese victory at Mukden, the Russians retreated. In October 1904 the Russian fleet, coming round from the Baltic, opened fire on a group of Hull fishing smacks in crossing the Dogger Bank, mistaking them for torpedo boats. The incident roused considerable indignation in Britain, but the Czar expressed his regrets. The matter was referred to a commission of admirals in Paris, and compensation was awarded for the damage done. On May 27, 1905 the Russian fleet was annihilated by Admiral Togo at Tsushima. The Japanese landed a force in Sakhalin, but, both sides being exhausted and anxious for peace, negotiations were opened in August 1905.

Political Result:

By the *Treaty of Portsmouth*, August 1905, the claims of Japan in Korea were recognized; Russia agreed to evacuate Manchuria and ceded the Liao-Tung peninsula (including Port Arthur) and the southern half of Sakhalin to Japan. The payment of an indemnity, which had been the chief obstacle to the conclusion of peace, was waived by Japan. The moderation of the Japanese demands made a good impression in the world, but was resented in Japan itself.

Remarks:

This was a war of pure aggression, backed by high financial speculation on the part of Russia. The easy triumph of Japan was a surprise. But she was fighting for definite national objects, while the Russian people knew nothing of the cause and aims of the war. Russia spent much money in subsequent years in restoring her lost armaments. From this time on the reform movements and revolutionary spirit in Russia grew rapidly.

TURKO-ITALIAN WAR

1911–1912

Belligerents:

> Italy.
> Turkey.

Cause:

After the agreements with regard to North Africa between Great Britain and France, Italy made up her mind that the time was favourable for a decisive move with a view to expansion, and proceeded to make careful preparations for military action early in 1911. The position in Tripoli was made the subject of heated discussion in the Press, and the Turks were charged with showing gross unfairness to Italian residents. The possible designs of Germany in North Africa also induced the Italian Government to take advantage of the first opportunity for an offensive step.

Occasion:

The Turks, foreseeing danger, sent war stores and munitions to Tripoli, and on September 29, 1911, the Italians, with their fleet ready and their troops embarked, declared war.

Course of the War:

On September 30th, Tripoli was blockaded and occupied by the Italians on October 5th; Benghazi fell on October 20th. In spite of the publication of a decree annexing Tripoli as a province of Italy, the advance of the invaders was kept in check. Austria refused to allow operations in the Adriatic. Russia would not permit the blockade of the Dardanelles. Fighting continued with indeterminate results and in a desultory manner until a treaty of peace was finally signed at Ouchy on October 15, 1912.

Result:

By the *Treaty of Lausanne*, October 15, 1912, Turkish forces were withdrawn from Tripoli and Cyrenaica, the Italians promised to withdraw from the occupied islands of the Ægean, and a commercial agreement was concluded between the two countries. There was no recognition by the Turkish Government of Italian sovereignty in

Tripoli. It was enough for Italy that her sovereignty was recognized by the Powers. This was done, France delaying her assent until Italy surrendered certain privileges in Morocco.

Remarks:

Italy's aggressive action was prompted by a desire not to be left behind in the competition for territorial acquisitions in Africa.

FIRST BALKAN WAR

1912–1913

Belligerents:

Serbia, Bulgaria, Greece, Montenegro.
Turkey.

Cause:

Even after the deposition of the Sultan, Abdul Hamid, and the triumph of the Young Turks in the revolution of 1908 the misgovernment of Turkey did not cease, more especially in Macedonia, where the European Powers had entirely failed to secure any reforms, but produced an intolerable situation in the Balkan Peninsula. Despairing of the successful intervention of the Powers the Balkan States determined to take matters into their own hands. For the first time an alliance was formed between Greece, Bulgaria, and Serbia for the purpose of destroying the Turkish Empire in Europe.

Occasion:

In September 1912 the Powers, through Austria, Hungary, and Russia strongly deprecated the outbreak of war. The Allies simultaneously handed in to the Turkish Government an Ultimatum demanding certain specified reforms. No reply was sent. The Turks underestimated the strength of their opponents, and hoped to detach Greece. War broke out October 17th.

Course of the War:

The Turkish forces were completely overwhelmed. They were defeated by the Serbians at Kumanovo, October 24, 1912, and Uskub was occupied: the Greeks drove the enemy north and occupied Salonika: and the Bulgarians defeated the Ottoman army at LuleBurgas, October 31st, and advanced to Chatalja. After an armistice and an abortive attempt of the Powers to secure peace, the war broke out again. Adrianople fell March 26, 1913, and the Turks submitted.

Political Result:

By the *Treaty of London* Bulgaria was given a frontier from Enos on the Mediterranean to Midia on the Black Sea. The future of Albania was to be decided by the Allies and Turkey ceded the island of Crete to Greece.

Remarks:

Serious disputes as to the disposal of the spoils won from Turkey led immediately to the outbreak of war among the Allies.

SECOND BALKAN WAR

1913

Belligerents:

Serbia, Greece, Montenegro, Roumania.
Bulgaria.
Turkey.

Cause:

In February 1912 a treaty was concluded between Bulgaria and Serbia, whereby it was agreed that North-west Macedonia should go to Serbia, another part to Bulgaria, and the zone lying between these two should be submitted to the arbitration of the Czar. In December 1912, in the First Balkan War, Austria protested against the occupation by Serbia of Durazzo on the Adriatic, and of Scutari by Montenegro. Serbia declared that Bulgaria did not adequately support her in resisting the Austrian demand, felt impelled to claim more territory in Macedonia, and refused to carry out the provisions of the treaty with Bulgaria. Serbia was ready to arbitrate. Russia was inclined to support the Serbian claim. Bulgaria hesitated.

Occasion:

While the dispute was still in the balance the aggressive party in Bulgaria got the upper hand, and war was declared against Serbia and Greece in June 24, 1913, only a few months after the cessation of hostilities in the First Balkan War.

Course of the War:

The Bulgarians found themselves invaded on four frontiers. While they were being driven back by Serbia and Greece, the Turks repudiated the Treaty of London and retook Adrianople, and Roumania advanced from the north and without striking a blow annexed a large slice of territory in the Dobrudja. Bulgaria was obliged to yield.

Political Result:

By the *Treaty of Bukarest*, August 10, 1913, Serbia acquired a large district of South-east Macedonia, Greece obtained Kavalla, and Roumania was given possession of the territory her troops had occupied.

By the *Treaty of Constantinople*, August 1913, Bulgaria ceded back to Turkey more than half of the territory won in the previous war, including Adrianople.

Remarks:

Bulgaria being again restricted in territory felt she had been betrayed by the Powers, who did nothing to enforce the engagements of the Treaty of London. Her rivals, Serbia and Greece, gained at her expense. On the other hand, Bulgarian responsibility for the outbreak of the second war was undoubted.

The European Powers, by acting together, prevented the Balkan conflict from spreading into a European War. But the Treaty of Bukarest was no settlement, and was a signal exposure of their inability to solve the Balkan problem, which was destined to be the spark for a world-wide conflagration.

IMPORTANT TREATIES

(OTHER THAN THOSE ALREADY MENTIONED)

The *Treaty of Vienna*, June 9, 1815.

Second Treaty of Paris, November 20, 1815, Signed by Great Britain, Austria, Prussia, Russia, France at the conclusion of the Napoleonic Wars.

France gave up certain fortresses on the frontier but retained Alsace-Lorraine. Payment of 700 million francs was exacted from France. The greater part of the Grand Duchy of Warsaw fell to Russia, Posen to Prussia, and Cracow became a republic. Prussia got back nearly all her old possessions, and there was a reconstruction of German States under a Confederation. Holland, Belgium, and Luxemburg were established as an independent kingdom under the House of Orange: Switzerland was extended and her integrity guaranteed: Sardinia obtained Genoa and other territory: Austria received an extension of territory in North Italy and on the coast of the Adriatic, and became the dominant state in the German Confederation. The Pope and the King of the Two Sicilies regained their former possessions.

[The foregoing record of wars serves to show to what a small extent this treaty secured the settlement of European territorial problems.]

The Rushe-Bagot Treaty, April 1817, between Great Britain and the United States. The two powers agreed to withdraw their battleships from the Great Lakes.

It may be noted that the absence of armaments on the whole Canadian frontier cannot be said to have endangered the relations between the two countries in view of the fact that the Anglo-American peace centenary was celebrated in 1915.

The Treaty of Washington, May 8, 1871, between Great Britain and the United States. The north-western boundary was finally delimited: an attempt was made to settle the Canadian Fishery dispute, and it was agreed to refer the Alabama Claims to a tribunal of arbitration, which subsequently fixed the sum to be paid over by Great Britain as indemnity.

The Triple Alliance in 1882 was the result of Italy joining the alliance between Germany and Austria, which had grown out of the support given to Austria as against Russia at the Congress of Berlin in 1878, Italy having become estranged from France after the occupation of Tunis in 1881. The Triple Alliance was renewed for five years in 1887 and in 1891, and again in 1902 it was extended for a term of twelve years.

The Berlin Act. The outcome of the Conference of Berlin, 1884–5, at which fourteen Powers were represented. The respective spheres of influence of the European Powers in Africa were delimited. The neutrality of the Congo Free State was recognized, and it was established as an independent State under the sovereignty of the King of the Belgians. An area was marked out in which there should be free trade, which should be excluded from effects of disputes between the signatory Powers, and be placed under the rule of neutrality.

The latter stipulation has, however, not been carried out.

The Suez Canal Convention signed by nine Powers at Constantinople, October 29, 1888. Lesseps obtained the preliminary concession for the construction of the Canal in 1856. The Canal was opened in 1869. Disraeli bought four million pounds' worth of shares from the Khedive on behalf of the British Government in 1875. The Convention ensured that the Canal should always be open to vessels of commerce and war without distinction of flag. Great Britain signed with a reservation, but in the Anglo-French agreement of 1904 declared her adherence to the Convention and agreed to its being put into force.

The Hay-Pauncefote Treaty, November 18, 1901, between Great
Britain and the United States, gave the United States
right of control in time of war of the Panama Canal.
The Clayton-Bulwer Treaty of 1850, which established
a joint Anglo-American protectorate over the Canal
was thereby abrogated.

The Anglo-Japanese Alliance. Treaties signed in London January
30, 1902, and August 12, 1905. The integrity and
independence of China was recognized. If either Great
Britain or Japan should be attacked and involved in a
war with two Powers, they engaged mutually to assist
one another. The aim of the alliance was officially
defined as "the consolidation and maintenance of
general peace in the regions of Eastern Asia and of
India." In 1911 the treaty was revised, a clause
stipulating that there was no obligation to go to war
with a Power with whom a treaty of arbitration was in
force. This removed the danger of Great Britain being
involved in a war between Japan and the United States.

The Argentine-Chile Treaty, 1902. From 1840 to 1900 constant
boundary disputes arose between the two countries,
which invariably led to war. At last the people
themselves in both countries decided by large
majorities to negotiate a peaceful settlement of the
dispute. The delimitation of the frontier was carried out
by a mixed commission, and to commemorate the
treaty an immense statue of Christ was erected on a
high pass in the Andes on the boundary line.

The Anglo-French Convention, April 8, 1904.

This removed outstanding causes of friction
between the two countries, and was the foundation of
the Entente.

Newfoundland fisheries and West African boundary
problems were settled: the Siamese, New Hebrides, and
Madagascar disputes were settled: Egypt was declared
exclusively under British protection, and Morocco was
left to France. A Franco-Spanish Convention was
concluded in October of the same year with regard to
Morocco. To both these treaties secret clauses were

attached which amounted virtually to the prospective partition of Morocco by France and Spain.

The Agreement of Karlstadt, September 23, 1905.

The Union between Sweden and Norway was dissolved, and Norway recognized as an independent kingdom.

The movement in favour of separation had grown rapidly from 1899. It was resisted by the King of Sweden. A plebiscite in Norway declared in favour of it, and agreement was reached without any armed conflict.

The Algeciras Act, April 7, 1906, agreed to by thirteen Powers, was based on the sovereignty, independence, integrity, and economic liberty of Morocco. The provisions concerned the organization of police, regulation of taxation, customs, etc. This Act was disregarded by France in 1911, when a French force was sent to Fez and occupied the country.

The Anglo-Russian Convention, September 23, 1907.

Persia was divided so as to give Great Britain and Russia spheres of influence with a neutral zone between. (Persia was not a party to the treaty.) An agreement was come to with regard to Afghanistan and Thibet, settling all points where dispute might arise.

The Anglo-American Arbitration Treaty, April 4, 1908.

By this Treaty differences between Great Britain and the United States which do not affect the vital interests, independence, or honour of either country, or which do not concern the interests of third parties are referred to the Permanent Court of Arbitration at the Hague.

BIBLIOGRAPHY

(Each war has its own literature. Only a few leading authorities and books easily accessible to students are given here.)

The Cambridge Modern History, vols. xi, xii.
Modern Europe. C. A. Fyffe.
A Political History of Contemporary Europe. Seignobos.
History of our own Times. Justin McCarthy.
A Century of British Foreign Policy. Gooch and Masterman.
History of our Time (1885–1911). G. P. Gooch.
Wars of the Nineties. Atteridge.
The Map of Europe by Treaty. Hertslet.
International Law. C. E. Hall.
The Termination of War and Treaties of Peace. Coleman Philipson.
Three Centuries of Treaties of Peace. Sir W. Philimore.
Turkey in Europe. Sir C. Eliot.
Nationality and War in the Near East. A Diplomatist.
The New Map of Europe. H. A. Gibbons.
Historical Atlas of Modern Europe. Robertson and Bartholomew.
The Balkan War. Lieut.-Col. Rankine.
History of the Greek Revolution. G. Finlay.
History of Italian Unity. Bolton King.
The Far Eastern Question. M. V. Chirol.
The History of South America. Akers.

The American Civil War. F. L.
Paxon.
The Downfall of Spain. Wilson.
The Invasion of the Crimea. A. W.
Kinglake.
Modern Egypt. Lord Cromer.
The War in South Africa. Hobson.
The War of Steel and Gold. H. N.
Brailsford.
Nationalism, War, and Society. E.
Krehbiel.
Ten Years of Secret Diplomacy.
E. D. Morel.
Imperialism. J. A. Hobson.
International Tribunals. Evans
Darby.

www.ingramcontent.com/pod-product-compliance
Lightning Source LLC
Chambersburg PA
CBHW020129180726
47992CB00020B/2564